The Personal or Group Study Guide to A.W. Tozer's *The Pursuit of God*

Jonathan L. Graf

CHRISTIAN PUBLICATIONS
CAMP HILL, PENNSYLVANIA

Acknowledgments

I wish to thank my Crossfire Care Group—Gene, Doreen, Valerie, Barb and Lisa—for allowing me to "test" this study on them. They provided valuable feedback. I also wish to thank the "Good News" class at Summerdale Alliance Church for putting up with another test run. They helped me to refine this study for use in larger groups. I would like to thank Dave Fessenden—my editor, who also sat in on the "Good News" class study—for providing helpful criticism. Even though I am also his boss, he had the courage to suggest the changes that were needed. Finally, I want to thank Rev. H. Robert Cowles for providing invaluable help as an "independent" set of eyes. The insights and input of all of these individuals have aided this study immensely.

Jonathan L. Graf

Contents

Christian Publications
3825 Hartzdale Drive, Camp Hill, PA 17011

The mark of ✝ *vibrant faith*

ISBN: 0-87509-504-6
© 1992 by Christian Publications
All rights reserved
Printed in the United States of America

92 93 94 95 96 5 4 3 2 1

How to Use This Guide

This study guide has been developed to help you get the most out of A. W. Tozer's classic *The Pursuit of God*. It should enable you to understand more clearly what Tozer is saying and to apply the truths he sets forth to your own life.

The study guide is designed for both personal and group use. The personal study section (the material that comes first in each session of this guide) should be read after you read the corresponding chapter in A. W. Tozer's *The Pursuit of God*. Let its comments and questions help you reflect on the major points Tozer is making. It will also provide you with additional Scripture to read and study. The group study section offers a lesson plan and discussion questions for those wishing to use *The Pursuit of God* as the text for an adult Sunday school class or a small group study.

Do not overlook the questions at the back of this study guide that go with each chapter. If you are using this guide by yourself, there should be space enough after each question for you to use that section as a work book. If you are leading a group study, you are hereby granted permission to make copies of the questions for your class members or group. (This permission is necessarily restricted to just the pages of questions in the back of the book.)

Personal Study

Whether you are studying personally or as the leader of a class or small group, you will want to begin by reading the personal study section of Session 1. It provides background information on both A. W. Tozer and how he came to write *The Pursuit of God.* Be sure to complete the "Introduction Questionnaire" you will find at the end.

From that point on, the best method of study will be to read thoughtfully a chapter from *The Pursuit of God,* answer the study guide questions corresponding to that chapter and then follow through with the related study guide lesson. Unless you are a group leader, you need not read the "LESSON PLAN— Group Study" section.

Group Study—Leader's Instructions

As you prepare for each session of your class or group, you will want to read the entire section of this guide that coincides with the chapter of *The Pursuit of God* that your group is studying. In other words, you need to read both the personal study section and the group lesson plans.

The group lesson plans are set up with the same subtitles used for the personal study. This is to help you find information quickly. When the activity recommends that you read a quotation from *The Pursuit of God,* that quotation usually is provided in the personal study section of this guide under the correlating subtitle. The personal study section will also suggest to you things of significance that you will wish to stress.

As we mentioned above, you are permitted to copy the study guide questions (they begin on page 86), one copy for each member of your group.

If some or all of your group are especially serious about this study, they may want to have their own copies of this study guide. Naturally, *all* members should have a copy of *The Pursuit of God* and keep up with the reading assignments. These lessons, however, are designed so that members who do not keep up with the reading assignments in *The Pursuit of God* can still get some benefit from the class.

Introduction

Supplementary Materials: *In Pursuit of God: The Life of A.W. Tozer*, James Snyder, Christian Publications, 1991; *How to Be Filled with the Holy Spirit*, A.W. Tozer, Christian Publications, n.d.; "Holy Spirit, Fill Me," Fred Hartley III, Christian Publications, 1992.

A.W. Tozer is one of the most-quoted Christian writers of the 20th century. In his period of highest visibility (1940s–1963) he was also one of the most sought-after speakers in evangelical circles. Because of his intimate relationship with God and his fearlessness at saying what God wanted him to say despite the potential unpopularity of his message, many called him a prophet. Chuck Swindoll has called him "the voice of evangelicalism."

At present, there are 39 A.W. Tozer books in print. Of those 39, only nine were produced while Tozer was alive. The remaining books are collections of editorials Tozer wrote while editor of *The Alliance Weekly/Witness* (now *Alliance Life*), or are compiled from his sermons. *The Pursuit of God* remains the all-time best-seller of Tozer's works. While official records have not been accurately kept (and many that were kept were lost in a flood in 1972), by conservative estimations, the English version of *The Pursuit of God* has sold over 1.2 million copies. The classic has also been translated into 19 languages.

In order to gain insight into the spiritual depth and strength of *The Pursuit of God*, it is important to look at who this man Tozer was, and how his classic came to be written.

Tozer, a Pursuer of God

Who was Aiden Wilson Tozer and what set him apart? What should we understand about him to aid us in our study? For a full appreciation of the man, you will want to read James Snyder's biography, *In Pursuit of God*.

Tozer was a man driven by a desire to know more of God. In fact he once said to his long-time friend, Robert W. Battles, "I want to love God more than anyone in my generation." To some of us that may sound selfish and arrogant, but for Tozer it wasn't. It simply came out of an honest desire to enrich his relationship with the Lord.

His humility and deep longing for God can be seen in his "Ordination Prayer." He wrote the prayer originally as a covenant with God at the time of his ordination to the Christian ministry, August 18, 1920. Later he revealed it to the world in one of his first editorials in *The Alliance Weekly*. A portion of it reads:

> Lord Jesus, I come to Thee for spiritual preparation. Lay Thy hand upon me. Anoint me with the oil of the New Testament prophet. Forbid that I should become a religious scribe and thus lose my prophetic calling. Save me from the curse that lies dark across the face of the modern clergy, the curse of compromise, of imitation, of professionalism. Save me from the error of judging a church by its size, its popularity or the amount of its yearly offerings. Help me to remember that I am a prophet—not a promoter, not a religious manager, but a prophet. Let me never become a slave to crowds.

Heal my soul of carnal ambitions and deliver me from the itch for publicity. Save me from bondage to things. Let me not waste my days puttering around the house. Lay Thy terror upon me, O God, and drive me to the place of prayer where I may wrestle with principalities and powers and the rulers of the darkness of this world. Deliver me from overeating and late sleeping. Teach me self-discipline that I may be a good soldier of Jesus Christ.

I accept hard work and small rewards in this life. I ask for no easy place. I shall try to be blind to the little ways that could make my life easier. If others seek the smoother path, I shall try to take the hard way without judging them too harshly. I shall accept opposition and try to take it quietly when it comes. Or if, as sometimes it falleth out to Thy servants, I should have grateful gifts pressed upon me by Thy kindly people, stand by me then and save me from the blight that often follows. Teach me to use whatever I receive in such manner that it will not injure my soul or diminish my spiritual power. (*In Pursuit of God,* pp. 58–59)

This drive to know God—to pursue God—often led Tozer to speak and preach on the subject of worship. When it came to worship, He despised the frivolous, the mundane and the shallow. And who could argue with him? He knew how to worship God. His biographer writes:

Once at a Bible conference [Tozer] testified to a spiritual experience he had as a young preacher. "A preacher friend joined me for a walk in the woods for private Bible reading and prayer. He stopped at a log and, if I know him, probably fell asleep. I went on a

little farther, as Jesus did, and knelt down and began to
read my Bible. I was reading about the camp of Israel
in the wilderness and how God laid it out in a beautiful
diamond pattern. All at once I saw God as I never saw
Him before. In that wooded sanctuary I fell on my face
and worshiped. Since that experience, I have lost all
interest in cheap religious thrills. The vacuous religious
choruses we sing hold no attraction for me. I came
face-to-face with the sovereign God, and since that time
only God has mattered in my life." (*In Pursuit of God*,
p. 161)

Others as well recognized the ability of Tozer to worship.
Raymond McAfee, his longtime associate at Southside Alliance
Church in Chicago, relates the following experience they had
when praying and worshiping together.

Tozer knelt by his chair, took off his glasses and laid
them on the chair. Resting on his bent ankles, he clasped
his hands together, raised his face with his eyes closed
and began: "Oh God, we are before Thee." With that
there came a rush of God's presence that filled the room.
We both worshiped in silent ecstasy and wonder and
adoration. I've never forgotten that moment, and I
don't want to forget it. (*In Pursuit of God*, p. 145)

The Writing of the Classic

Every writer has a different method to make the creative juices
flow. Some discipline themselves to write several hours a day;
some need to get away and write for a solid week or two; some
use a special writing pad, typewriter or computer. Tozer was to
become a disciplined writer, particularly when he became editor
of *The Alliance Weekly* and had the responsibility of producing

an editorial for every issue. But in 1948, the year he gave birth to his classic, he was not yet into those disciplined rigors. True, he had written two biographies, *Wingspread*, about Albert B. Simpson, the founder of The Christian and Missionary Alliance, Tozer's own denomination, and *Let My People Go*, about pioneer missionary R.A. Jaffray (both books are still in print). But Tozer didn't think of himself as a writer—he was a pastor. In fact, Tozer had a very different view as to when a person should write. James Snyder, in his biography, quotes him on the subject: "The only book that should ever be written is one that flows up from the heart, forced out by . . . inward pressure. . . . You should never write a book unless you just have to" (*In Pursuit of God*, pp. 121–122). It was just such pressure that produced the book you are about to study.

Tozer had a speaking engagement in McAllen, Texas, a town near the Mexican boarder. Air travel in the spring of 1948 was not yet commonplace, so he boarded an overnight sleeper for the rail trip to McAllen.

At the time, Tozer was struggling with a "burden" God had given him. He was concerned about the apparent shallowness of many believers—people who claimed to be followers of Christ but who had little knowledge of God and little desire to know Him better. Somehow he wanted to motivate these people.

Upon boarding the train, Tozer asked the porter for a small writing table. And secluded in his sleeper compartment he began to write—oblivious of all else.

About nine in the evening the porter announced the last call for dinner. Tozer asked him for some tea and toast and he kept on writing. As he wrote, the words fairly tumbled into his mind. Feverishly he put them down on paper. By morning he had the entire draft of the book that would affect millions of people to this day (see *In Pursuit of God*, pp. 124–125).

None of Tozer's other books were written in quite this same manner. And although his other books have had a very good ministry, none has come close to the success of *The Pursuit of God.*

Your Relationship with God

That is a thumbnail sketch of A.W. Tozer and the writing of his classic *The Pursuit of God.* Does the "burden" that prompted Tozer to write his book find a response in your heart? What about your relationship with God and His Son Jesus Christ? Would you like it to be closer, more intimate? Why not pause right now and ask God to use His own Word, *The Pursuit of God* and this study you are beginning to effect a powerful, lasting change within you.

The Apostle Paul says: "Examine yourselves to see whether you are in the faith; test yourselves. Do you not realize that Christ Jesus is in you—unless, of course, you fail that test?" (2 Corinthians 13:5). In another place he says, "continue to work out your salvation with fear and trembling, for it is God who works in you to will and to act according to his good purpose" (Philippians 2:12–13).

It is important that we continually take stock of our relationship with the Lord—not because we are worried about losing our salvation, but because a relationship that isn't growing is a stagnant relationship and a hindrance to the work of God.

Before you begin *The Pursuit of God* and follow through this study, take stock by answering the following questions as honestly as you can. You may want to write down your answers—and then review the questions a few weeks after you complete this study to see how your answers may have changed. (Note: this same questionnaire heads the study work sheets at the back of this guide.)

1. How does one become a Christian?

2. When did I become a Christian?

3. Did becoming a Christian bring any noticeable changes to my life? What were they?

4. Have I ever had a subsequent experience that I would consider to be the filling of the Holy Spirit? When did it happen? What changes did this experience bring in my life?

5. Do I find joy in worshiping God, both privately and with fellow believers?

6. How often do I gather with other believers?
   a. less than weekly
   b. weekly
   c. twice a week
   d. more than twice a week

7. How often do I read my Bible?
   a. never
   b. seldom
   c. once or twice a week
   d. three to five times a week
   e. daily or oftener

8. How often do I converse with God in prayer?
   a. seldom
   b. once or twice a week
   c. three to five times a week
   d. daily
   e. frequently throughout the day

9. When I pray is it a meaningful time of communion, or do I quickly run through a list of requests?

10. When a problem occurs in my life, what is my first response to it?
    a. pray or ask "what is God trying to teach me?"
    b. immediately turn the matter over to God
    c. think "what am I going to do?"
    d. react emotionally
    e. do nothing

11. If I answered c, d or e to question 10, how soon do I get around to a or b?
    a. very quickly
    b. somewhat soon
    c. not very soon
    d. never

Improving Your Relationship

As you go through this study, you will be confronted with principles that affect your relationship with God. A most crucial starting point is your prayer life. What did you answer to questions 8 and 9? Unless you're a well-above-average Christian, you may not have scored very high on those two questions. Yes, you pray, but has your prayer life been really meaningful? Have you felt as though you were actually communing with God? Tozer will be introducing the idea of drawing near to God. The concept comes from the letter to the Hebrews:

> Therefore, brothers, since we have confidence to enter the Most Holy Place by the blood of Jesus, by a new and living way opened for us through the curtain, that is, his body, and since we have a great high priest over

the house of God, *let us draw near to God* with a sincere heart in full assurance of faith, having our hearts sprinkled to cleanse us from a guilty conscience and having our bodies washed with pure water. Let us hold unswervingly to the hope we profess, for he who promised is faithful. (10:19–23, italics added)

James speaks in similar terms: "Come *near to God* and he will come near to you" (4:8a, italics added). But what does nearness mean? Is it the amount of time—the *quantity*? Or is it the *quality* of the interaction?

On a visit to Hong Kong, an American businessman had occasion to ride the subway. The trains were so crowded, he said, that certain employees were on the platforms just to push people into the cars so the doors could close. The American said he was jammed against people on all sides of him—he was "closer" to more people than he had ever been before. Yet they were all strangers; he did not know them. He was not really "near" any of them.

That may typify your relationship with God. You are close in proximity to Him but you do not really know Him. You go through motions, perhaps praying for a list of requests you read off to God. And probably you take time to quickly scan a few verses or a chapter from the Scriptures. Quite likely you are in church regularly. But you do not feel "near" to God in the sense of intimately knowing Him.

Concerning prayer, someone has suggested that most of us have our focus all wrong. We glance at God and gaze at our needs. Rather we should be gazing at God and glancing at our needs. If we want to develop a meaningful prayer life, we must focus on God and not on the peripherals.

This week, why not try relating God's Word back to Him when you pray? Often referred to as "praying the Scriptures," this is a good discipline that helps us focus on God. It also allows God to speak to us. You might start with one of the Psalms— Psalm 103 is a good one to begin with. Begin by simply, prayerfully reading a verse or phrase—changing the "his"-"he" pronouns to "Your" and "You" and the "your"-"you" pronouns to "my" and "me." Then if thoughts come to your mind and heart to be added, voice them. For example, you might begin Psalm 103:1 by praying:

> Praise the LORD, O my soul;
>   all my inmost being praises Your holy name.

> Father God, teach me to praise You more with my inner being, my mind, my soul. Cause my praise to come from deep within me. Do not let me be superficial with You.

Then move on to verse 2. You may not want to pray this way all the time, but see if it doesn't bring a deeper sense of intimacy into your prayer life. Your focus will turn from a "prayer list"—gazing at needs—to the Supplier—gazing at God.

Why not end this first study by taking such a passage from the Scriptures and praying through it?

LESSON PLAN—Group Study

AIM: To cause my students to examine their own relationships with God and to desire to draw nearer to Him.

Tozer, a Pursuer of God

1. Explain Tozer's passion for wanting to know God. It would be a good idea to read the quotes that are provided earlier.

2. After reading Tozer's statement about wanting to love God more than anyone else loves Him, ask: What do you think about making such a statement? Was it a prideful or humble remark? Would you dare to say that? Why or why not?

3. After reading about Tozer's experiences with the presence of God you may want to ask: Can any of you relate a time when you profoundly felt the presence of God?

The Writing of the Classic

1. Pass out copies of *The Pursuit of God.*

2. Explain the circumstances surrounding the writing of the book. You will want to say everything you can to convince your class members that they should read the book chapter by chapter, in its entirety. As we said, the lesson plans are designed so that a student who has not read the assigned chapter can get *something* out of each session, but those who thoughtfully, prayerfully read all that Tozer has to say will derive maximum benefit.

Your Relationship with God

1. If time permits, spend a few minutes looking at the chapter titles in the table of contents.

2. To stimulate discussion, ask: What chapters especially intrigue you? Why?

3. Pass out copies of the "Introduction Questionnaire." [Copy from back of study guide, or type up your own questionnaire based on the one provided.] Allow 10 minutes for class members to complete it. Depending on the intimacy level of your group, you may want to invite sharing on some of the questions.

4. Discuss Hebrews 10:19–22 and James 4:8. Consider together what it means to be "near to God." Relate the Hong Kong subway illustration.

5. Explain the concept of focus in our prayer life—gazing at God rather than at our needs.

6. You may want to open the class up and ask students what they do in their prayer time to focus on God. Present the idea of "praying the Scriptures." If there is time, have them turn to Psalm 103 and practice praying in this manner. Depending on the size of your class or group, you may want to have the members divide up into two or more smaller groups. Make sure no one feels pressured to pray aloud. Such a person can simply read the verse when it is his or her turn and at the end say "Amen."

Closing
1. Assign Tozer chapter 1 to be read before the next meeting, and pass out the study guide sheet for chapter 1. To whet the appetites of your members, you may want to read an incisive quote from the chapter.

2. Close in prayer.

Tozer Chapter 1

Following Hard after God

Supplementary Materials: *"Weak Thing" in Moni Land*, William Cutts, Christian Publications, 1990.

Do you have a desire to know God better? The very fact that you arereading *The Pursuit of God* and using this study guide indicates to some extent that you want to experience more in your relationship with God. But our desires are often confused and muddy. *What is God's role in developing my desire? How much work do I have to do to improve our relationship?* Chapter 1 in *The Pursuit of God* deals with these questions.

One question is answered in a theological term we call *prevenient grace*. What does prevenient grace mean? Basically this: before a person can seek God, God must first have sought the person. In other words, God puts within us the impulse to pursue Him. It wouldn't be there without the Holy Spirit of God first working to place that desire or urge within our souls (read John 6:44).

But, while it is the Holy Spirit who puts that urge within us, we still have a responsibility: to pursue God. It is our job to do the pursuing (read First Chronicles 16: 10–11; Psalm 9:10).

The Need to Pursue

Tozer points out that while it is refreshingly true that our justification is by faith, there is often a problem with our "easy conversions" of today. A person can be "saved" by mechanically saying a simple prayer. "Christ can be 'received' without creating any special love for Him in the soul of the receiver. The man is 'saved,' but he is not hungry nor thirsty after God. In fact he is specifically taught to be satisfied and is encouraged to be content with little" (pp. 12–13).

How do we get to know someone? By spending time with him or her. You can't get to know someone personally and intimately through one visit. Likewise you must spend time with God if you are to get to know Him intimately. What, according to Tozer, is the essence of genuine religion? Read John 17:3.

Tozer goes on to say:

> God is a person, and in the deep of His mighty nature He thinks, wills, enjoys, feels, loves, desires, and suffers as any other person may. In making Himself known to us He stays by the familiar pattern of personality. He communicates with us through the avenues of our minds, our wills and our emotions. The continuous and unembarrassed interchange of love and thought between God and the soul of the redeemed man is the throbbing heart of New Testament religion.
>
> This intercourse between God and the soul is known to us in conscious personal awareness. It is personal: it does not come through the body of believers, as such, but is known to the individual, and to the body through the individuals which compose it. It is conscious: it does not stay below the threshold of consciousness and work there unknown to the soul (as, for instance, infant

baptism is thought by some to do), but comes within
the field of awareness where the man can know it as he
knows any other fact of experience. (pp. 13–14)

Are you personally, consciously aware of God? Would you
like to be?

This Intimate Relationship Is Personal

Tozer points out that this conscious awareness, this intimate
relationship cannot come through a body of believers. Why
can't this relationship come through our involvement with a
body of believers? What are the benefits of being a part of a body
of believers? (List some of them.)

While there are many benefits to being a part of a body of
believers, too many people substitute their association with a
group for an actual, intimate relationship with God. Again if
you do not have a personal, intimate relationship with God, you
can. Tozer points out that everyone should come to a point in
his or her faith where he or she is as aware of God as he or she
knows any other fact of experience. If this isn't your experience,
may God use this study to bring you into such an awareness of
Himself.

Salvation Only Begins Our Pursuit

Very many believers stop their pursuit at salvation. "Yes, I
believe in God and I have accepted Jesus Christ as my personal
Savior, but I'm satisfied with that." If only we can encourage
those that there is much more of God to experience. A limitless
God means there is no end to our pursuit of Him! What a
paradox that is: to know God and yet still to pursue Him!

Two examples of individuals who knew God well were Moses
and Paul. Yet, both had a strong desire to know more of
God—neither was satisfied with his level of knowledge. Read

Exodus 33:13–18. These verses show to what lengths Moses went in order to know God more fully. Read Philippians 3:4–14 and ponder Paul's desire.

The Lack of Spiritual Growth

What is deadly to spiritual growth? Read again what Tozer says:

> I want deliberately to encourage this mighty longing after God. The lack of it has brought us to our present low estate. The stiff and wooden quality about our religious lives is a result of our lack of holy desire. Complacency is a deadly foe of all spiritual growth. Acute desire must be present or there will be no manifestation of Christ to His people. He waits to be wanted. Too bad that with many of us He waits so long, so very long, in vain.
>
> Every age has its own characteristics. Right now we are in an age of religious complexity. The simplicity which is in Christ is rarely found among us. In its stead are programs, methods, organizations and a world of nervous activities which occupy time and attention but can never satisfy the longing of the heart. The shallowness of our inner experience, the hollowness of our worship, and that servile imitation of the world which marks our promotional methods all testify that we, in this day, know God only imperfectly, and the peace of God scarcely at all.
>
> If we would find God amid all the religious externals, we must first determine to find Him, and then proceed in the way of simplicity. Now, as always, God discovers Himself to "babes" and hides Himself in thick darkness from the wise and the prudent. We must simplify our

approach to Him. We must strip down to essentials (and they will be found to be blessedly few). We must put away all effort to impress, and come with the guileless candor of childhood. If we do this, without doubt God will quickly respond. (pp. 17–18)

For many of us this complacency and lack of acute desire is the root cause of our lack of significant spiritual growth. Some cover up this inner complacency by looking for outward solutions: "My church isn't vibrant enough," "My pastor doesn't preach the Word with power," and so on. Then they look for a more "exciting church" with a more "dynamic" pastor, but that isn't the solution to their lack of spiritual growth.

Tozer pointed out (p. 18) that many search for *God-and.* It is the "ands" that we need to strip away. Tozer felt we need to simplify our approach to God. Read Matthew 18:3–4. Remember that God reveals Himself to "babes" and hides Himself from the wise. We need a simple faith; a simple trust with no strings attached. We need to retain that childlike trust throughout our relationship with the Lord.

One of the most profound examples of simple faith comes from *"Weak Thing" in Moni Land,* the autobiography of William A. Cutts, former missionary to the Moni people of Irian Jaya.

Ototome, a young Moni man from Dugindoga Valley was visiting the Beoga Valley, being entertained in the home of one of the locals. Just as a guest in the States might help the hostess by drying the dishes, Ototome went to the woods to get some firewood. There he was struck on the back by a falling tree. He later told us that his back had been broken. The new Christian Damals who were with him said, "No problem. We'll pray for you and the Chief of Heaven will answer our prayers and heal you." They prayed and Ototome got up and walked back to the hut.

"What sort of thing is this new talk about the Chief of Heaven and His Son?" he wondered. "It has power—not at all like our spirit-appeasement ceremonies where we give all that we have and get nothing in return."

While Ototome was still in the Beoga, messengers came to tell him that his little son had contracted diarrhea and was getting weaker and weaker. Again, the new Damal Christians said, "Don't get upset. The Chief of Heaven has power to heal your boy. We will pray for him right now and he will be well again."

Ototome immediately headed home with the messengers, trekking as fast as possible, hoping to see his son still alive. He was amazed when he saw the boy, not lying listlessly in his mother's lap, but out in the village yard playing with friends. Just as the Beoga Christians had prayed. The news of this double miracle spread through the Dugindoga Valley like wildfire. (pp. 135–136)

That God honors simple, uncomplicated faith, there is no doubt. Lord, help our faith and trust to become less complicated and to focus solely on You.

We need to approach God like the author of the old classic, *The Cloud of Unknowing*. "Lift up thine heart unto God with a meek stirring of Love; and mean Himself, and none of His goods. And thereto, look thee loath to think on aught but God Himself. So that nought work in thy wit, nor in thy will, but only God Himself. This is the work of the soul that most pleaseth God" (pp. 18–19). Too often we approach God hoping for an experience or a sensation instead of simply wanting only

God. Try seeking God Himself alone.

LESSON PLAN—Group Study

AIM: To cause my students to examine their own desire to pursue God.

Introduction

1. Open with prayer.

2. Using the questions provided on page 15 of the personal section, discuss God's role in developing our desire to seek Him. Have students read the Scripture verses listed and then discuss them.

The Need to Pursue

1. Discuss what Tozer meant by "easy conversions."

2. Discuss the questions provided under "The Need to Pursue."

3. Read the Tozer quote on pages 13 and 14. Ask: "Are you personally, consciously aware of God? Would you like to be?" Discuss.

This Intimate Relationship Is Personal

1. Using the questions from "This Intimate Relationship Is Personal," discuss why a personal relationship cannot come through a body of believers. List the benefits of being a part of a body of believers.

2. Discuss the fact that we should come to a place in our spiritual life where we are as aware of God as we are of any other

fact of experience. Discuss what keeps us from this intimacy—
sin.

Salvation Only Begins Our Pursuit

1. Discuss questions provided under this subhead in the personal study section.

2. Read and discuss Scripture provided.

The Lack of Spiritual Growth

1. Ask: "What is deadly to spiritual growth?" Read the Tozer
quote on pages 17 and 18. Discuss.

2. Discuss the problem of "church hoppers."

3. Discuss the concept of "God-and." Read Scripture
provided.

4. Read the passage provided from *"Weak Thing" in Moni
Land.* Discuss the passage in relation to the concept of "simple
faith."

Closing

1. Read together Tozer's prayer at the end of his chapter 1.

2. Assign reading of Tozer chapter 2 and hand out study guide
questions .

3. Close in prayer.

Tozer Chapter 2

The Blessedness of Possessing Nothing

Supplementary Materials: *In Pursuit of God: The Life of A. W. Tozer*, James Snyder, Christian Publications, 1991.

A.W. Tozer had a somewhat unusual interpretation of Matthew 5:3. He did not take "poor in spirit" to mean those who are sad and depressed, but rather those who do not let things—possessions—be too important. In fact, they are people who do not even consider their things to be theirs, but God's.

To these "poor in spirit" people, nothing is theirs—nothing they have comes before God in importance to them. This is a very difficult concept to understand. It is even more difficult to allow God to control you totally.

You can say, "Oh, I have turned everything over to the Lord and He controls my life and my things." But do you really practice that? If we knowingly hold back anything, we are still in control. We can say, "But God controls 95 percent of my life, so He is really the One who is in control." Not true. If we are holding anything back, then we are in control, for when we say, "God, you can have 95 percent of me; I'll just hold on to this 5 percent," we are actually saying that we are still the one who decides what to give and what not to give—we are the controller. Possess nothing! Give it all to the Lord for His control!

Giving God Control

To understand this idea, and to support Tozer's view of Matthew 5:3, read and think about Genesis 22:1–18. How does the story of Abraham and Isaac support Tozer's view?

Tozer himself had a struggle similar to Abraham's. His biographer relates this:

> In 1939, Ada Tozer gave birth to a girl, Rebecca. After six rambunctious boys and a nine-year hiatus, in their middle years the Tozers joyfully welcomed Becky into their home and hearts. Years later, in a sermon, Tozer reflected on that momentous event: "She was a lovely little thing. After raising six boys—it was just like trying to bring up a herd of buffaloes—this refined, feminine little lady came along with all her pretty, frilly things. She and I became sweethearts from the very first day I saw her little red face through the glass in the hospital. I was 42 years old when she was born."
>
> Tozer went on to tell how they dedicated Becky to the Lord. "We dedicated her formally in the church service, but she was still mine. Then the day came when I had to die to my Becky, my little Rebecca. I had to give her up and turn her over to God to take if He wanted her at any time. . . . When I made that awful, terrible dedication I didn't know but God would take her from me. But He didn't. . . . She was safer after I gave her up than she had ever been before. If I had clung to her I would have jeopardized her; but when I opened my hands and said with tears, 'You can have her, God,

the dearest thing I have,' she became perfectly safe." (*In Pursuit of God*, pp. 187–188)

Why is clinging to things one of the most harmful habits in life? What are some things that are hard for people to give up? What things are hard for you to give up? The story is told about a pastor—it may have been Peter Marshall—who was discussing giving with one of his parishioners. The man had at one time been of modest means, yet a great giver. Now he was rich and he found it difficult to give. He commented to his pastor that giving the same percentage of money now that he used to give simply amounted to too much money. His pastor said, "I think I understand your problem; let's pray about it." Then he proceeded to pray: "Oh Lord, please make this man poor again so he can enjoy the blessing of giving."

You get the point—the more we have, the harder we hold on to it. Statistics show that those who give the highest percentage of their income to charity make less than $20,000 per year. But let's look at what Scripture says about our possessions and their relation to our walk with God.

Scripture to Study

Read Matthew 19:16–30. What does this passage teach about possessing things? Does it teach we have to sell everything we have? How do we give up the things that possess us? What does this passage teach about the "What's in it for me?" attitude so prevalent today?

Read Mark 8:34–38. What truths can be gleaned from this passage that relate to our theme?

Read Luke 9:57–62. What does this passage teach about serving God only when it is convenient for us? What does it teach about our home and family? How does a "home" possess us and become wrong?

Read Luke 12:15–34. What does this passage say about the following topics: life and possessions; storing up our treasures; anxiety and our provisions?

Read Luke 14:26–35. How should you look at your life? Do things control you—wealth, family, etc.—and keep you from God? Would you still follow God if He allowed something precious to you to be taken away, or would you become angry and bitter?

Conclusion

Reread Tozer's prayer on pages 30 and 31. Can you honestly pray this prayer? What choice are you going to make? What choice does God want you to make?

LESSON PLAN—Group Study

AIM: To cause students to see the relationship between our possessions and our walk with God. To encourage students to "give up" their possessions to God.

Introduction

1. Discuss Tozer's interpretation of Matthew 5:3.

2. Discuss what it means for God to have full control of our lives. Be sure to emphasize the fact that if we knowingly hold anything back from God, we are still in total control of our lives.

Giving God Control

1. Read Genesis 22:1–18. (Note: if you are certain that everyone in your group is familiar with the story, reading the entire passage is not necessary.)

2. Discuss how the story of Abraham and Isaac supports Tozer's view.

3. Read the quote on pages 28 and 29 of this study guide about Tozer's difficulty in "giving up" his daughter. Use the questions following the quote for discussion.

Scripture to Study

1. Have the group discuss each passage. If you have a large group, this is a good opportunity to break up into smaller teams. Have each team study and report on a passage. The questions following each passage can be copied and given to each group.

Closing

1. Have your class turn to Tozer's prayer on pages 30–31 of *The Pursuit of God*. This prayer is one of the most intense in the book. You may not want to have everyone read it together out loud because many will not mean it! Instead you might ask for a time of silent meditation, recommending that those who mean it pray the prayer silently; others may want to simply pray for the courage to make that decision to "give up" their possessions to God.

2. Hand out the study guide questions and assign the reading of chapter 3.

3. Close in prayer.

Tozer Chapter 3

Removing the Veil

"Thou hast formed us for Thyself, and our hearts are restless till they find *rest* in Thee."—Augustine

Hebrews 10 tells us, "Therefore, brothers, since we have confidence to enter the Most Holy Place by the blood of Jesus, . . . let us draw near to God with a sincere heart in full assurance of faith, having our hearts sprinkled to cleanse us from a guilty conscience and having our bodies washed with pure water" (verses 19, 22). But while we *should* have confidence and we *should* enter into God's presence, few Christians do. Why is that? Why do so many of us settle for far less spiritually than we could have? Remember what Tozer said:

> The world is perishing for lack of the knowledge of God and the church is famishing for want of His presence. The instant cure of most of our religious ills would be to enter the Presence in spiritual experience, to become suddenly aware that we are in God and that God is in us. This would lift us out of our pitiful narrowness and cause our hearts to be enlarged. (p. 38)

Perhaps the very fact that you are studying *The Pursuit of God* indicates that you have a longing within you to know more of God—a desire to enter His presence. So what steps should you take?

Glorify God

Begin by glorifying God. That is why man was created—to glorify God. Read Revelation 4:11. How do you glorify God? The following are some ways in which we can glorify God. Look up each verse and meditate on it.

- Psalm 86:11-12—walking in truth
- Romans 15:5-6—unity of the body
- 1 Corinthians 6:20—our bodies
- 2 Corinthians 9:13—obedience to our confession of the gospel (following the Word)
- 1 Peter 2:12—keeping life pure, good deeds before non-Christians
- 1 Peter 4:16—suffering
- 1 Corinthians 10:31—whatever we do
- Psalm 115:1—by praising God for what He does and who He is

Take a moment to praise God for His character and His attributes. Meditate on the meanings and implications of *eternal, immutable, omniscient, love, mercy, righteousness* and *holiness.*

Our Position

Why do so many find the Christian life a struggle? Why do so many find it difficult for praises to roll off the tongue? Maybe we don't feel we have anything to praise God for. Name some things which you can praise God for.

Removing the Veil

Read Hebrews 9:1–14; 10:19–23. Meditate on the implications of these passages. We now can enter the Holy Place—the
very presence of God.

Tozer was a solid evangelical believer, yet he is often labeled
as a modern mystic. He loved reading the mystics and even
compiled a collection— *The Christian Book of Mystical Verse—*
of their writings. One of the reasons he loved the mystics was
because they seemed to understand this removal of the veil.

> They were prophets, not scribes, for the scribe tells us
> what he has read, and the prophet tells what he has seen.
> The distinction is not an imaginary one. Between the
> scribe who has read and the prophet who has seen there
> is a difference as wide as the sea. We are overrun today
> with orthodox scribes, but the prophets, where are they?
> The hard voice of the scribe sounds over evangelicalism,
> but the church waits for the tender voice of the saint who
> has penetrated the veil and has gazed with inward eye
> upon the wonder that is God. And yet, thus to penetrate,
> to push in sensitive living experience into the holy
> Presence, is a privilege open to every child of God. (p. 43)

According to Tozer, many of us are stuck in the outer courts.
So why don't we enter His presence? What hinders us? Sin—
particularly the sin of self. Purity is very important to our
personal communion with the Almighty God.

In the Old Testament, before the High Priest entered the
Most Holy Place—and that but once a year—a sacrifice had to
be made to purify him. In fact, such was the importance of this
that tradition has it that the priest would have a rope tied around
him when he went into the Most Holy Place. This was so his
body could be pulled out if he was struck dead for approaching

God with uncleanness.

And so there is still a "veil" in front of us hiding God's presence from us:

> It is the veil of our fleshly, fallen nature living on, unjudged within us, uncrucified and unrepudiated. It is the close-woven veil of the self-life which we have never truly acknowledged, of which we have been secretly ashamed, and which for these reasons we have never brought to the judgment of the cross. (p. 44)

We must say—*and mean*—Lord, remove the veil. Take my self-love—my flesh—and remove it. But that is difficult. According to Tozer, this self-love is the thread from which this inner veil is woven. This is the reason it is so hard to tear down: the hyphenated sins of self are not something we *do*, they are something we *are*. "Therein," says Tozer, "lies both their subtlety and their power."

> To be specific, the self-sins are self-righteousness, self-pity, self-confidence, self-sufficiency, self-admiration, self-love and a host of others like them. They dwell too deep within us and are too much a part of our natures to come to our attention till the light of God is focused upon them. The grosser manifestations of these sins—egotism, exhibitionism, self-promotion—are strangely tolerated in Christian leaders, even in circles of impeccable orthodoxy. They are so much in evidence as actually, for many people, to become identified with the gospel. I trust it is not a cynical observation to say that they appear these days to be a requisite for popularity in some sections of the church visible. Promoting self under the guise of promoting Christ is

currently so common as to excite little notice. (p. 45)

Tozer goes on to say that this veil can only be removed in spiritual experience, never by mere instruction. Unfortunately, our problem often is that we wait for instruction. We want instruction. But if we would only *do*! Take heart, God will do the work if we want it done! Our part is to yield and trust. Do we have the courage to let go of all the hidden "hyphenated selfs"?

> Insist that the work be done in very truth and it will be done. The cross is rough and it is deadly, but it is effective. It does not keep its victim hanging there forever. There comes a moment when its work is finished and the suffering victim dies. After that is resurrection glory and power, and the pain is forgotten for joy that the veil is taken away and we have entered in actual spiritual experience the presence of the living God. (p. 47)

LESSON PLAN—Group Study

AIM: That my students will see that they can confidently enter God's presence. They will learn some of the hindrances to entering.

Introduction
1. Open with prayer.

2. Read the quote from page 38 of *The Pursuit of God.* Discuss the issue of entering with confidence into God's presence.

Glorify God
1. Discuss why man was created. Read Revelation 4:11.

2. Have individuals read the verses provided under the personal guide subhead "Glorify God." Have the reader of each verse explain the way in which the verse indicates we can glorify God.

3. Take time to praise God for His character and His attributes.

Our Position

1. Discuss why so many Christians find life a struggle, and why so many find it difficult for praises to roll off the tongue. Take time to think of things we can praise the Lord for.

Removing the Veil

1. Have someone read Hebrews 9:1–14 and 10:19–23. Discuss the implications of these verses.

2. Discuss the lives of some who obviously "enter the veil." Have students name people they know or use Tozer's quote about the "mystics." For extra help, use *The Christian Book of Mystical Verse* compiled by Tozer (Christian Publications).

3. Discuss the hindrances to entering God's presence (sin, lack of desire). Use the quotes provided in the personal guide about the sin of self.

Closing

1. Read the prayer on page 47 of *The Pursuit of God* together.

2. Hand out study guide questions and assign the reading of Tozer chapter 4.

3. Close in prayer.

Tozer Chapter 4

Apprehending God

An important step in improving our relationship with God is to analyze just what our level of belief in God is. As a start to that analysis, reread Tozer pages 50 and 51.

Level of Belief

Are you clear as to the differences between knowing God as an inference, an ideal or as a reality known in personal experience? Where do you think you are in the area of belief?

One of the major problems in Christianity today is that so many Christians say they believe in the reality of God but in actuality they only believe in God as an inference or ideal. Meditate on what Tozer says:

> Christians, to be sure, go further than this, at least in theory. Their creed requires them to believe in the personality of God, and they have been taught to pray, "Our Father, which art in heaven." Now personality and fatherhood carry with them the idea of the possibility of personal acquaintance. This is admitted, I say, in theory, but for millions of Christians, nevertheless, God is no more real than He is to the non-Christian.

They go through life trying to love an ideal and be loyal to a mere principle. (p. 50)

God as a Reality

To understand God as a reality, it would be helpful to think about why the unregenerated man can't apprehend God. Read First Corinthians 2:14 and Romans 1:20–21. Meditate on the implications of these verses.

Now think about the ways you know God in reality. Perhaps list the experiences you remember where God showed Himself to you.

How can the Christian know God? He or she should be able to know God in the same way that he or she knows the reality of this world. Read the following verses and reflect on the sense that is mentioned: Psalm 34:8; 45:8; John 10:27; Matthew 5:8.

Next it is important to remember that God brings life to the believer—and an ever-deepening awareness of Himself to those who *want* to grow in faith. That word *want* is important to our spiritual growth and our growing awareness of God. The importance of possessing a free will does not end with salvation. If we do not exercise our free will and decide we want to grow, to know more of God, then we won't grow.

For further study in this area of knowing God as a reality, read and meditate on the following verses: Romans 8:10; 1 Corinthians 2:6–16; Ephesians 2:1–7, 5:14; Hebrews 9:14.

The Key of Faith

Remember that the key to developing our spiritual senses is faith. Read Hebrews 11:6. It is also important to understand Tozer's point about the difference between faith and imagination. Projecting unreal images out of the mind and seeking to attach reality to them is imagination. But that is not faith. Faith does not create anything; it simply believes—Tozer used the word *reckons*—on that which is already there.

Faith believes in the world invisible to us. Why is it so easy to believe in the world we can see and doubt the one we can't see? Read Second Kings 6:8–17.

Are there cases today of God's giving special "sight" to see His armies? The following comes from *On Call*, a missionary auto-biography by Dr. David Thompson. It takes place in Cambodia in the early 1950s during the French-Indochina War.

> We had been in Kratie for perhaps a year. French troops were garrisoned in the city because it was a provincial capital. One day the French commander received secret information that a large force of rebels was going to attack the French rubber plantations outside of the town of Snoul, 80 kilometers away. Confident that his information was correct, the commander loaded his troops on trucks and raced to Snoul, hoping to surprise the rebels. The purported attack never materialized. It was a rebel trick.
>
> The actual plan was for a rebel force of about 2,000 to attack Kratie where we lived. As dusk fell, a soldier knocked on our door and asked if we would like to come to the hotel where they were planning to fight to the finish. Father thanked him, but said no. Instead, he said, he and his wife would pray. God had not brought them to Kratie to be destroyed before they had done the work they were sent to do.
>
> I remember having to stay under the bed with my sister while Dad and Mom knelt and prayed. Mom said we were very fussy and made it hard for them to pray. As Dad told it, around 2 a.m. a white flare lit up the square between our house and the hotel. The attack on the hotel started soon after.

Bullets flew everywhere. Suddenly, a red flare shot up and burned briefly in the night sky. The shooting tapered off. In the morning there was no sign of the rebels and nobody understood why the rebels had abandoned the attack. The French commander returned later that day from Snoul and was surprised to find the city intact.

In 1955 the French granted independence to Cambodia, returning power to the king of Cambodia. The king promised amnesty to all the rebels who would turn in their weapons and pledge allegiance to him—some of the rebels were communists. On the announced day, the provincial rebels came by the thousands to the town square and stacked their weapons in a great pile. There were speeches and ceremonies all day. Towards the middle of the day, the retiring French commander asked Dad to translate for him while he spoke to the rebel commander. After the introductions, the commander asked the rebel leader, "Why did you not take the city the night we were diverted to Snoul, leaving Kratie defenseless?"

The rebel commander seemed surprised by the question. He remembered the night very well, he said, and suggested that the French commander was mistaken, for when the rebels attacked Kratie they were confronted by thousands of French soldiers. There were troops everywhere—more than he had seen at any other time during the war! Since the rebel force numbered only 2,000 men, they had decided to flee.

With Dad interpreting, the French commander and the rebel leader argued about the events of that night. Only Dad understood what had happened: the army of the Lord had saved us. God's angels had appeared as

French soldiers in such great numbers that the rebels withdrew. (pp. 17–19)

If we truly seek to follow Christ, we need to be "other-worldly." For Tozer, that means for us to reshift our focus.

If we would rise into that region of light and power plainly beckoning us through the Scriptures of truth, we must break the evil habit of ignoring the spiritual. We must shift our interest from the seen to the unseen. For the great unseen Reality is God. "He that cometh to God must believe that he is, and that he is a rewarder of them that diligently seek him" (Heb. 11:6). This is basic in the life of faith. From there we can rise to unlimited heights. "Ye believe in God," said our Lord Jesus Christ, "believe also in me" (John 14:1). Without the first there can be no second. (pp. 56–57)

We need to rise above circumstances and see the Glory of God. May God help us to do so.

A great help in this area of faith and apprehending God is another Tozer book, *Christ the Eternal Son* (Christian Publications), a collection of sermons on the book of John, compiled after Tozer's death.

LESSON PLAN—Group Study

AIM: That my students will learn the concept of thinking "other-worldly."

Introduction
1. Open in prayer.

Level of Belief

1. Begin by discussing the levels of belief in God as presented on pages 49–50 of *The Pursuit of God.*

A. **To most people God is an inference, not a reality.** They deduce that He must exist but He is not spiritually known to them.

B. **To others God is only an ideal.** He is "goodness," "beauty," "truth" or "the creative impulse behind existence."

C. **God is a reality known in personal experience.**

2. Discuss the problem that many Christians say they believe in the reality of God but in actuality they believe in God as an inference or ideal.

3. Read and discuss the Tozer quote from page 50 provided in the personal guide section.

God as a Reality

1. As an encouragement to the weaker members of the class, use Study Guide Question 1. Have members share the ways they know that God is a reality. Spend as much time as possible here since this exercise might be the most beneficial part of the class for those who struggle with their faith.

2. Discuss the unregenerate man—Why can't he apprehend God? Look at First Corinthians 2:14 and Romans 1:20–21. Discuss the deadness of man, how that affects his ability to understand God.

3. Discuss how the Christian can know God. He or she should be able to know God in the same way that he or she knows the reality of this world. Use verses that show the use of the senses: Psalm 34:8; 45:8; John 10:27; Matthew 5:8.

4. God brings life to the believer—then an ever-deepening awareness to those who want to grow in faith. Select some (or all) of the following verses to discuss: Romans 8:10; 1 Corinthians 2:6–16; Ephesians 2:1–7, 5:14; Hebrews 9:14.

The Key of Faith

1. The key to developing our spiritual senses is faith. Read Hebrews 11:6.

2. Discuss Study Guide Questions 5 (the difference between imagination and faith) and 6 (why we think of the visible world as real and often doubt the other).

3. Read and discuss Second Kings 6:8–17. Elisha had spiritual sight that allowed him to see the hosts of God.

4. Do such things still happen today? Yes! Read the experience from *On Call,* by Dr. David Thompson, son of later martyred missionaries, Ed and Ruth Thompson.

5. What do we have to be if we truly seek to follow Christ? Discuss what it means to be "other-wordly." Read the quote from Tozer page 57. Discuss what that means and what the implications are. Perhaps read the paragraph that begins on the bottom of page 57: "If we would rise . . . there can be no second."

Closing

1. Read the prayer on Tozer page 59, together.

2. Hand out the study guide questions and assign chapter 5 to read for next week.

3. Close in prayer.

Session 6

Tozer Chapter 5

The Universal Presence

When contemplating God's presence and what the "Universal Presence" means, we may find it easy to misunderstand the implications. Tozer points this out in his discussion of pantheism vs. God's presence.

The Divine Presence

If you are hazy as to the distinctions between the two views, review pages 61 and 62. Tozer talks about "the divine immanence" or the fact that God dwells in His creation and is everywhere individually present in all His works. This is *not* pantheism, which is the belief that God is the *sum* of all created things. "The truth is," says Tozer, "that while God dwells in His world He is separated from it by a gulf forever impassable. However closely He may be identified with the work of His hands, they are and must eternally be other than He" (p. 62).

The important aspect we want to meditate on in our study is, *What implications about the presence of God are here for us personally? How can we benefit in our personal relationship with the Lord Jesus Christ through an increased awareness and knowledge of the "Universal Presence"?*

Begin by reading Psalm 139:7–10. As a contemplation exercise rewrite the verses in your own words, substituting places and situations that are meaningful to you.

Remember, God knows everything! He is everywhere! At no time—ever—are we away from the presence of God! That should be an encouragement to us! (There is also an implication to ponder: you can possibly fool fellow Christians about who and what you are, but not God!)

Read and meditate on these other verses: 1 Kings 8:27; Acts 17:27–28.

Sensing God's Presence

Of course this raises the question: Why don't we sense God's presence? Tozer responds to this by saying:

> The Presence and the manifestation of the Presence are not the same. There can be the one without the other. God is here when we are wholly unaware of it. He is manifest only when and as we are aware of His presence. On our part, there must be surrender to the Spirit of God, for His work is to show us the Father and the Son. If we cooperate with Him in loving obedience, God will manifest Himself to us, and that manifestation will be the difference between a nominal Christian life and a life radiant with the light of His face. (p. 64)

The issue of being fully surrendered and obedient to Him cannot be stressed enough. Tozer rightly points out that these areas are the difference between nominal Christian living and a radiant Christian life. Remember from Session 1 when we discussed the difference between nearness of place and nearness of relationship? We must strive to be near in relationship to the Lord if we want to have a deeper experience of His presence.

Tozer points out that we can pray for an increasing degree of awareness. "It will be a great moment for some of us," he states, "when we begin to believe that God's promise of self-revelation is literally true, that He promised much, but no more than He intends to fulfill" (p. 65).

Spiritual Receptivity

Think about this question: Why do some Christians experience God in a way that others do not?

Tozer indicates that it is something called "spiritual receptivity." Within those who truly want more of God and truly sense His presence, a spiritual awareness is cultivated! It is developed until it becomes the biggest thing in their lives. Read Psalm 27:8. Do you, like David, truly seek God's presence with your whole heart? The important issue here is that when you feel an inner longing, you *do something about it!*

Did you understand Tozer's definition of what this receptivity is? He says it is a compound thing, a blending together of several elements within the soul—a knowledge of doctrine and theology intermingled with experience. It is "an affinity for, a bent toward, a sympathetic response to, a desire to have." The fact that you are seriously studying this book indicates that you have such a desire. Cultivate it!

And how is that desire cultivated? Tozer says that it is increased by exercise and destroyed by neglect! He also points out that our ignorance of this fact "is the cause of a very serious breakdown in modern evangelicalism."

> The idea of cultivation and exercise, so dear to the saints of old, has now no place in our total religious picture. It is too slow, too common. We now demand glamour and fast flowing dramatic action. A generation of Christians reared among push buttons and automatic machines is impatient of slower and less direct methods

of reaching their goals. We have been trying to apply machine-age methods to our relations with God. We read our chapter, have our short devotions and rush away, hoping to make up for our deep inward bankruptcy by attending another gospel meeting or listening to another thrilling story told by a religious adventurer lately returned from afar. (p. 69)

And how can we break out of a life of dull spiritual senses? Turn to God in earnest! We have within us the ability to know Him if we would only respond to His overtures!

What a difference a simple heart attitude can make. When you approach a Sunday morning thinking, *Oh well, it's another Sunday and I've got to go to church. I wonder how long the service will go today.* That is not the way to meet God—unless He drives you to an altar of repentance because of your lousy attitude! But when you go to church with the heartfelt anticipation of being in God's presence and with the excitement of another opportunity to worship God with fellow believers, you can expect Him to meet you with an outpouring of His presence. Approach God with desire!

LESSON PLAN—Group Study

AIM: To help my students realize a deeper understanding of God's presence and to cultivate the desire within them to develop their spiritual awareness.

Introduction
1. Open in prayer.

The Divine Presence
1. Discuss the differences between a biblical understanding of

God's universal presence and pantheism.

2. Read Psalm 139:7–10. Ask some students to share their rewritten Psalm according to the instructions in Study Guide Question 2.

3. Discuss the implications God's universal presence has to our own lives.

Sensing God's Presence

1. Read and discuss the Tozer quote from page 64 of *The Pursuit of God.*

2. Discuss why so many Christians seldom sense His presence.

Spiritual Receptivity

1. Discuss what Tozer meant by "spiritual receptivity."

2. Discuss how it is developed and how it is hindered.

3. Read the Tozer quote from his page 69.

4. Discuss ways to break out of spiritual dullness.

Closing

1. Read together the prayer on Tozer page 71.

2. Assign chapter 6 to read and hand out study guide questions for next week's class.

3. Close in prayer.

Tozer Chapter 6

The Speaking Voice

Supplementary Materials: *70 Years of Miracles*, Richard H. Harvey, Horizon House Publishers, 1977, 1992. *You Can Make a Difference*, Tony Campolo, Word Books, 1984.

Does God still speak today? Tozer would shout a resounding "Yes!" Are you aware of God's speaking voice in your own life? Try to recall a time when you were certain the Lord was speaking to you. If you need more encouragement, read *70 Years of Miracles*, which is loaded with true stories of miraculous answers to prayer and instances of God's clearly speaking to people. Tony Campolo's book *You Can Make a Difference* also has a wonderful story of God's clearly speaking to His people (pp. 24–25).

When pondering this issue of God's speaking, it is important to understand how to hear His voice. In what forms does it come? Can we develop an ear for it?

God's Voice in His Word

One way to hear God's voice is to read His Word—the Bible. Read Psalm 33:6, 9; Hebrews 11:3; Genesis 1:9. What do these verses indicate about the power of God's Word?

What is the relation of God's spoken Word to His written Word—the Bible? To understand this issue, study what Scripture says about God's Word.

A. Jeremiah 5:14, 23:29; Ephesians 6:17; Hebrews 4:12
B. 1 Peter 1:23–2:3
C. Psalm 119:89; Matthew 24:35
D. Deuteronomy 8:3; Job 23:12; Psalm 119:103
E. Psalm 119:11; Deuteronomy 11:18; Romans 10:8; Colossians 3:16
F. Jeremiah 15:16; Psalm 119:140
G. Psalm 19:8, 119:105, 130; Proverbs 6:23; 2 Peter 1:19

God's Voice to the Unsaved and the Saved

The Scriptures indicate that God's voice is apparent to the unsaved. Read John 1:9–10; Romans 1:20; 2:15. What do these verses have to say about God's voice and the unsaved?

God's voice is also apparent to His children in the same ways plus many more ways as well. But we have to tune our ear to it. And that is difficult. As Tozer said:

> Whoever will listen will hear the speaking Heaven. This is definitely not the hour when men take kindly to an exhortation to listen, for listening is not today a part of popular religion. We are at the opposite end of the pole from there. Religion has accepted the monstrous heresy that noise, size, activity and bluster make a man dear to God. But we may take heart. To a people caught in the tempest of the last great conflict God says, "Be still, and know that I am God" (Ps. 46:10), and still He says it, as if He means to tell us that our strength and

safety lie not in noise but in silence. (p. 80)

Do you allow enough times of stillness in your life to hear the voice of God? Sometimes we are afraid to be still because we're not sure about God's voice. How did you know it was God's voice that you heard? One sure test is that God will never tell us something that is contrary to His Word, the Bible! If you are not sure it was God's voice you heard, check out what you heard against Scripture. Meditate on His Word—He will give you the certainty you need.

Developing Your Sense of Hearing

Do you want to hear more of God's voice? There are ways yourcan develop your sense of hearing so you can more closely and regularly hear God's voice:

1. The first and most obvious way is to be still and listen. Establish more silent time as a part of your devotional life.
2. Second, obey God's Word. Allow the Bible to be "a living Book" to you. Deal with the sin in your life. Keep your life pure before God. Develop your spiritual ears through spiritual exercise. Increase your times of Bible reading and prayer.
3. Finally, pray for illumination. At the beginning of each quiet time, ask the Holy Spirit to speak to you. Remember what Tozer said:

It is important that we get still to wait on God. And it is best that we get alone, preferably with our Bible outspread before us. Then if we will we may draw near to God and begin to hear Him speak to us in our hearts. I think for the average person the progression will be something like this: First a sound as of a Presence walking in the garden. Then a voice, more intelligible, but still far from clear. Then the happy moment when the Spirit begins to illuminate the Scriptures, and that which had been only a sound, or at best a voice, now becomes an intelligible word, warm and intimate and clear as the word of a dear friend. Then will come life and light, and best of all, ability to see and rest in and embrace Jesus Christ as Saviour and Lord and All. (pp. 80–81)

As a closing exercise, read Psalm 29 and meditate on God's voice.

LESSON PLAN—Group Study

AIM: That my students will learn the characteristics of God's spoken and written Word and understand how to develop their "ears" to hear God's spoken voice.

Introduction
1. Open with prayer.

2. Find an illustration to use as an example of God's clearly speaking to an individual. Two suggestions are given at the beginning of the personal study.

God's Voice in His Word
1. Have students read Psalm 33:6, 9; Hebrews 11:3; and Genesis 1:9. Discuss what they say about God's Word.

2. Discuss the relationship between God's spoken Word and His written Word, the Bible.

3. Assign the following verses to students. Have them explain what each says about God's Word.

A. (Powerful): Jeremiah 5:14, 23:29; Ephesians 6:17; Hebrews 4:12
B. (Purifies): 1 Peter 1:23–2:3
C. (Eternal): Psalm 119:89; Matthew 24:35
D. (Food): Deuteronomy 8:3; Job 23:12; Psalm 119:103
E. (Should be written on our hearts): Psalm 119:11; Deuteronomy 11:18; Romans 10:8; Colossians 3:16
F. (We should love it): Jeremiah 15:16; Psalm 119:140
G. (Brings light): Psalm 19:8, 119:105, 130; Proverbs 6:23; 2 Peter 1:19

God's Voice to the Unsaved and the Saved

1. Discuss how God's voice is apparent to the unsaved. Read John 1:9–10, Romans 1:20 and 2:15.

2. Discuss the ways in which God's voice is apparent to His children.

3. Read the Tozer quote from page 80. Discuss the importance of stillness in hearing God's voice.

4. Have students share times when they heard God's voice. Discuss how they knew it was God's voice. Bring out the point that God will never tell us to do something that is contrary to His written Word!

Developing Your Sense of Hearing

1. Discuss the ways we can develop our ability to hear God's voice.

A. Be still and listen. Establish more silent time as a part
    of your devotional life.
B. Obey God's Word. Allow the Bible to be "a living
    Book" to you. Deal with the sin in your life. Keep
    your life pure before God.
C. Develop your spiritual ears through spiritual exercise.
    Increase your times of Bible reading and prayer.
D. Pray for illumination.

2. If time permits, read Psalm 29 and discuss what it tells us
about God's voice.

Closing

1. Read together the prayer on pages 82–83 of *The Pursuit of
God.*

2. Assign Tozer chapter 7 to read and hand out the study guide
questions for next week.

3. Close in prayer.

Session 8

Tozer Chapter 7

The Gaze of the Soul

And without faith it is impossible to please God, because anyone who comes to him must believe that he
exists and that he rewards those who earnestly seek him.
(Hebrews 11:6)

WHat is faith? Hebrews 11:1 tells us that "faith is being
sure of what we hope for and certain of what we do not
see." And what do we have if we have faith? According to Tozer
our faith allows us to approach God; through it we have
forgiveness, deliverance, salvation, communion and our
spiritual life.

Faith Defined
There is an important dimension to faith that we must not
miss. Tozer tells us that faith is defined functionally, not
philosophically. What did he mean by that? There is a clue in
Hebrews 11:1, for this verse shows faith in operation, not in
essence. What might that imply about faith? Just that faith is
proven in action.
Study the following verses in Hebrews 11: 4, 5, 7, 8, 11, 17,
20, 21, 22, 23, 29 and 31. Notice that we are told each

individual did something "by faith." When there is faith, there is an action.

Study these other Scriptures that talk about faith, and notice in each passage what action results from faith: James 2:14–26; Ezekiel 33:32; Matthew 7:21; 1 John 3:11–18. We can safely conclude that if there isn't a demonstration of faith in our lives, we cannot say we have faith.

Obtaining Faith

How do we obtain faith? Read Ephesians 2:8 and Romans 10:17. What do they reveal about how faith is obtained?

To understand faith in action, read Numbers 21:4–9. Compare this with John 3:14–15. What does this teach us about faith today? Tozer points out that "looking" in the Old Testament and "believing" in the New are the same thing! Israel looked with external eyes. Believing is done with the heart and mind. Faith is the gaze of the soul upon a saving God. Compare Psalm 34:5 and Psalm 123:1–2 with Matthew 14:19 and John 5:19–21. What do these verses say to us about faith?

Hebrews 12:2 tells us that we are to look—"fix our eyes"—to gaze with our soul, to believe, to have faith. For our faith to increase, our gaze needs to increase. Tozer tells us that faith is not a once-done act—it is a continuous gaze of the heart at God.

Believing, then, is directing the heart's attention to Jesus. It is lifting the mind to "behold the Lamb of God," and never ceasing that beholding for the rest of our lives. At first this may be difficult, but it becomes easier as we look steadily at His wondrous person, quietly and without strain. Distractions may hinder, but once the heart is committed to Him, after each brief excursion away from Him, the attention will return again and again and rest upon Him like a wandering bird coming back to its window.

I would emphasize this one committal, this one great volitional act which establishes the heart's intention to gaze forever upon Jesus. God takes this intention for our choice and makes what allowances He must for the thousand distractions which beset us in this evil world. He knows that we have set the direction of our hearts toward Jesus, and we can know it too, and comfort ourselves with the knowledge that a habit of soul is forming which will become, after a while, a sort of spiritual reflex requiring no more conscious effort on our part. (pp. 90–91)

My grandfather is a very good illustration of what Tozer is saying here. My grandfather loved the Lord. He was a long-time pastor, from the old school. Having become a believer when he was an adult, Grandpa never went to Bible college or seminary, yet he knew God and how to communicate to people. I remember fondly the times I spent with him when I was a young boy. Grandpa had an interesting quirk. Often we would be doing something together—playing caroms was a favorite pastime— and Grandpa would get this faraway look in his eye. He would then lean back in his chair, sigh contentedly and say, "Well, bless the Lord!" As a boy I didn't understand fully what he was doing. But now I see. Grandpa had such a rich love for the Lord Jesus Christ and such a deep faith in Him that whenever his mind wandered from what he was doing, it wandered to the things of the Lord! That was the spiritual reflex of faith that Tozer talked about—a faith so rich and strong that our minds simply wander to thoughts of God whenever they wander.

Tozer goes on to add that "like the eye which sees everything in front of it and never sees itself, faith is occupied with the Object upon which it rests and pays no attention to itself at all.

. . . Faith is a redirecting of our sight, a getting out of focus of our own vision and getting God into focus" (p. 91).

Remember, too, that faith doesn't need props. It can be exercised in any season, at any time and in any place.

Strengthening Our Gaze

What purifies and strengthens our gaze? Bible reading, prayer and corporate worship. We all accept spending more time in Bible reading and prayer as a means of deepening our faith, but what about corporate worship? While our relationship with God is personal, Tozer indicates that the development of individual faith does something to the unity of the body of Christ—it strengthens it! What a wonderful illustration is provided on page 96:

> Has it ever occurred to you that one hundred pianos all tuned to the same fork are automatically tuned to each other? They are of one accord by being tuned, not to each other, but to another standard to which each one must individually bow. So one hundred worshippers meeting together, each one looking away to Christ, are in heart nearer to each other than they could possibly be were they to become "unity" conscious and turn their eyes away from God to strive for closer fellowship. Social religion is perfected when private religion is purified.

We need more believers who "gaze their souls" on God and not on externals.

LESSON PLAN—Group Study

AIM: That my students will learn that the proof

of faith is action.

Introduction

1. Open with prayer.

2. Read Hebrews 11:6 and 11:1. Discuss what faith is.

Faith Defined

1. Discuss what Tozer means by faith being defined functionally and not philosophically.

2. Have students read the verses provided in Hebrews 11 and point out in each what the action was.

3. Study the other provided Scriptures and discuss what each says about the action of faith. James 2:14–26 (Faith without works is dead. If there isn't a demonstration of our faith, how can we say that we have faith?); Ezekiel 33:32 (Action demonstrates our true heart!); Matthew 7:21 (Only those who do the will of My Father); 1 John 3:11–18 (Love is the mark; action is the proof).

Obtaining Faith

1. Have students read Ephesians 2:8 and Romans 10:17. Discuss how we obtain faith.

2. To discuss faith in action, compare Numbers 21:4–9 with John 3:14–15. What do they teach us about faith today?

3. Discuss the comparison of "looking" in the Old Testament with "believing" in the New. Read and discuss Psalm 34:5; Psalm 123:1–2; Matthew 14:19; John 5:19–21; Hebrews 12:2.

4. Read the Tozer quotes from pages 90 and 91.

Strengthening Our Gaze

1. Discuss the things that strengthen our "gaze."

2. Discuss the importance of faith to the unity of corporate worship. Use the quote from page 96.

Closing

1. Read the prayer on page 97 of *The Pursuit of God* together.

2. Assign Tozer chapter 8 and hand out the study guide questions for next week.

3. Close in prayer.

Tozer Chapter 8

Restoring the Creator-Creature Relation

In order to think about the Creator-creature relationship and restoring it to its intended position, we must understand the effects of that relationship that the Fall left.

Fallen and Restored Humanity

Tozer indicates that the Fall left a radical moral dislocation, an upset in our relation to God and each other. So dislocated did our relationship with God become that we no longer even realized that it is only a proper relationship with the Creator that can bring true happiness.

What are we like apart from our relationship with God? Study Romans 1:20–32. Pay particular attention to verse 25.

After pondering fallen humanity, think about restored humanity. And what restores the Creator-creature relationship? "Essentially," says Tozer, "salvation is the restoration of a right relation between man and his Creator, a bringing back to normal of the Creator-creature relation." Read Second Corinthians 5:17.

A Fixed Center

Tozer talked about the importance of "a fixed center

against which everything else is measured." Why should
God be our fixed center?

> In determining relationships we must begin some-
> where. There must be somewhere a fixed center against
> which everything else is measured, where the law of
> relativity does not enter and we can say "IS" and make
> no allowances. Such a center is God. When God would
> make His name known to mankind He could find no
> better word than "I AM." When He speaks in the first
> person He says, "I AM"; when we speak *of* Him we say,
> "He is"; when we speak *to* Him we say, "Thou art."
> Everyone and everything else measures from that fixed
> point. "I am that I am," says God, "I change not."
> As the sailor locates his position on the sea by "shoot-
> ing" the sun, so we may get our moral bearings by
> looking at God. We must begin with God. We are right
> when, and only when, we stand in a right position
> relative to God, and we are wrong so far and so long as
> we stand in any other position.
> Much of our difficulty as seeking Christians stems
> from our unwillingness to take God as He is and adjust
> our lives accordingly. We insist upon trying to modify
> Him and to bring Him nearer to our own image. (pp.
> 100–101)

What does he mean that "we modify" God? In what ways do
we? Tozer says the only thinkable relation between us and God
is one of full Lordship on His part and complete submission on
our part! Why is that important?

Read and meditate on Job 38:1–38, 40:1–2; compare with
Job's response in 40:3–5, 42:1–6. For further study read and
meditate on the following: Daniel 4:28–37; James 4:6; Proverbs

16:5, 18:12.

What does it mean to be humble and submit to the Creator-God?

Developing the Proper Relationship

Tozer next points out that "we must of necessity be servant to someone." What does he mean? What is the proof of what or whom we are serving? Tozer indicates that it is the choices we make day after day.

> Our break with the world will be the direct outcome of our changed relation to God. For the world of fallen men does not honor God. Millions call themselves by His name, it is true, and pay some token respect to Him, but a simple test will show how little He is really honored among them. Let the average man be put to the proof on the question of who or what is *above*, and his true position will be exposed. Let him be forced into making a choice between God and money, between God and men, between God and personal ambition, God and self, God and human love, and God will take second place every time. Those other things will be exalted above. However the man may protest, the proof is in the choices he makes day after day throughout his life. (pp. 102–103)

The question arises then: How is a proper Creator-creature relationship developed? By truly exalting and honoring God. Tozer points out: " 'Be thou exalted' is the language of victorious spiritual experience." Read First Samuel 2:30. Think about the lives of Abraham, Jacob, David, others. They did not possess perfection, but rather their "holy intention," their attitudes toward God made the difference.

Whom Do We Honor?

We have to be very careful *whom* we honor! Read John 5:44 and then meditate on the following:

> ... Christ taught here [John 5:44] the alarming doctrine that the desire for honor among men made belief impossible. Is this sin at the root of righteous unbelief? Could it be that those "intellectual difficulties" which men blame for their inability to believe are but smoke screens to conceal the real cause that lies behind them? Was it this greedy desire for honor from man that made men into Pharisees and Pharisees into Deicides? Is this the secret back of religious self-righteousness and empty worship? I believe it may be. The whole course of the life is upset by failure to put God where He belongs. We exalt ourselves instead of God and the curse follows. (pp. 106–107)

It is important to give God His proper honor. Do not give honor due Him to men. Do not take honor due Him for yourself. One way we can develop this proper relationship with the Creator-God is to praise and exalt Him more. Make such praise a part of your devotional life.

Worship and Praise

As an exercise in praise, read aloud the following passages of Scripture that exalt God: Psalm 57:5–11; Philippians 2:9–11; Psalm 36:5–9; Psalm 33:1–12; Psalm 8:1–9; Psalm 94:1–9; Psalm 104:1–35; Psalm 93; Revelation 5:9–14.

LESSON PLAN—Group Study

AIM: That my students will understand what the Fall

did to the Creatore-creature relationship. They will also learn what a proper relationship is and how to develop it.

Introduction

1. Open with prayer.

2. Ask the class: What effect did the Fall have on the Creator-creature relationship?

Fallen and Restored Humanity

1. Continue discussing fallen humanity. Read Romans 1:20–32. Discuss what these verses say about the unregenerated person.

2. What restores our relationship with our Creator? Read 2 Corinthians 5:17. Discuss the implications of being new creations in Christ.

A Fixed Center

1. Discuss the importance of a fixed center. Why should God be our center?

2. Read the Tozer quote from pages 100–101.

3. Discuss what Tozer meant by saying that we attempt to "modify" God.

4. Discuss the issue of complete Lordship. Compare and discuss Job 38:1–38 and 40:1–2 with Job 40:3–5 and 42:1–6. Also look at Daniel 4:28–37; James 4:6; Proverbs 16:5; Proverbs 18:12.

5. Discuss the importance of humility and submission in a right relation with God.

Developing the Proper Relationship

1. Discuss what Tozer says is the proof of whom we are serving—our every day choices. Read his quote from pages 102–103.

2. Discuss how a proper Creator-creature relationship is developed.

Whom Do We Honor?

1. Discuss whom we honor. Read John 5:44 and Tozer's quote from pages 106–107.

Worship and Praise

1. If time allows have members of your class read the following Scripture passages that exalt God (you might have them share their favorites as well): Psalm 57:5–11; Philippians 2:9–11; Psalm 36:5–9; Psalm 33:1–12; Psalm 8:1–9; Psalm 94:1–9; Psalm 104:1–35; Psalm 93; Revelation 5:9–14.

Closing

1. Read the prayer on page 108 of *The Pursuit of God* together.

2. Assign Tozer chapter 9 to read and hand out the study guide questions for next week.

3. Close in prayer.

Tozer Chapter 9

Meekness and Rest

Blessed are the meek, for they will inherit the earth.
(Matthew 5:5)

What do you think it means to be meek? So often we hear that word and we think wimp or fearful or shy. In the chapter you have just read, Tozer uses the beatitudes and the Sermon on the Mount as a backdrop to discussing meekness. Read Matthew chapters 5, 6 and 7. Meditate on the type of persons we ought to be according to these chapters.

Now compare what Tozer said:

> In the world of men we find nothing approaching the virtues of which Jesus spoke in the opening words of the famous Sermon on the Mount. Instead of poverty of spirit we find the rankest kind of pride; instead of mourners we find pleasure seekers; instead of meekness, arrogance; instead of hunger after righteousness we hear men saying, "I am rich and increased with goods and have need of nothing"; instead of mercy we find cruelty; instead of purity of heart, corrupt imaginings; instead of peacemakers we find men quarrelsome and resentful;

instead of rejoicing in mistreatment we find them fighting back with every weapon at their command. (pp. 109–110)

All our heartaches—and many physical ills—come directly from our sins: pride, arrogance, resentfulness, evil imaginings, malice, greed, etc. Read Matthew 22:37–40. Why do you think Christ said that all other commandments rest on these? If we truly loved our neighbor as ourself what would that eliminate? Study Exodus 20 and see which commandments would not be a problem if we loved our neighbor.

What Is Meekness?

Now go back to meekness and see what Jesus and the Bible said about it. Study the following verses and try to decipher its qualities: Luke 6:29; 1 Peter 2:23; Galatians 5:22–23; 2 Timothy 2:25; Titus 3:2; 1 Peter 3:4. Study these verses to discover some promises: Psalm 37:11, 147:6, 149:9.

Meekness and Rest

Now to tie together both qualities talked about in the chapter, meditate on Matthew 11:28–30. What burden is Tozer talking about?

How about rest? The word Jesus uses here means: "a load carried or toil borne to the point of exhaustion." Meditate on the following verses that speak about rest: Exodus 33:14; Psalm 55:6, 116:7. Rest is simply release from that burden. It is not something we do—it is what comes when we cease to do!

Think about the burdens that weigh us down.

1. Pride—the burden of self-love

Why is pride a burden? What does it cause us to do? We will take affront at people who say something about us. We get hurt at the slightest thing. It is tough to have inner peace when we fiercely try to protect ourselves. Remember, God wants to relieve us of the burden of caring what other people say.

But does that mean we should never stand up for ourselves? Does being "meek" mean we are to be doormats? No! As Tozer reminds us:

> The meek man is not a human mouse afflicted with a sense of his own inferiority. Rather, he may be in his moral life as bold as a lion and as strong as Samson; but he has stopped being fooled about himself. He has accepted God's estimate of his own life. He knows he is as weak and helpless as God has declared him to be, but paradoxically, he knows at the same time that he is, in the sight of God, more important than angels. In himself, nothing; in God, everything. That is his motto. He knows well that the world will never see him as God sees him and he has stopped caring. He rests perfectly content to allow God to place His own values. He will be patient to wait for the day when everything will get its own price tag and real worth will come into its own. Then the righteous shall shine forth in the Kingdom of their Father. He is willing to wait for that day. (p.113)

2. Pretense—the burden of pretending

What does pretense mean? (pretend, make-believe). Pretentious? (showy, pompous, claim a knowledge we don't have). It is the common human desire to put the best foot forward and hide from the world our real inward poverty. It causes us to think we are better than others. There is an added burden in Christian circles: We put on a spiritual front, often allowing our inner weaknesses to stay hidden.

But what does the Bible say? That we are to come as little children.

3. Artificiality—the burden of hiding

This burden is deadly because we fear that some day we will be careless and someone will be allowed to, as Tozer puts it, "peer into our empty souls."

> Another source of burden is *artificiality*. I am sure that most people live in secret fear that some day they will be careless and by chance an enemy or friend will be allowed to peep into their poor, empty souls. So they are never relaxed. Bright people are tense and alert in fear that they may be trapped into saying something common or stupid. Traveled people are afraid that they may meet some Marco Polo who is able to describe some remote place where they have never been. . . . Artificiality is one curse that will drop away the moment we kneel at Jesus' feet and surrender ourselves to His meekness. (p. 115)

How do we get rid of these burdens and accept Christ's rest? We must surrender. We must recognize our complete dependency on Him. Read Second Corinthians 12:9–10. Are you allowing Him to be the strength in your life? Have you surrendered yourself at Jesus' feet?

You may discover a large source of "rest" by meditating on Second Samuel 22:29–37, particularly verses 34–37. Read this passage. The encouragement comes in realizing that while God never promises to keep us from trials, He does promise to supply and equip us for the trials. Verse 34 tells us that God doesn't remove the obstacles, but He does give us the energy to jump over them. Verse 35 tells us that He doesn't keep us out of battle but He does train us for it. Verse 37 tells us that He gives us the sure-footedness we need to walk on any path. What an encouragement to just rest in Him!

Many of us are trying to preserve a comfortable, easy Christianity, when deep down we are suffering from these burdens. But we are too afraid to let them go. We need to turn them over to the Lord, saying: "I recognize my spiritual poverty, my pride and artificiality. God, do a work in my life; I am turning these burdens over to you!" Don't be afraid—just trust. God may shake you up, but He will do the best thing for you!

LESSON PLAN—Group Study

AIM: To cause my students to understand what biblical meekness is and to learn how to rest in God.

Introduction

1. Open with prayer.

2. Read the beatitudes in Matthew 5.

3. Discuss the type of persons we ought to be according to these verses. Compare Tozer's quote from pages 109–110.

4. Read Matthew 22:37–40. Discuss why Christ said all commandments rest on these two. Compare the Ten Commandments (Exodus 20). How is Christ's statement true?

What Is Meekness?

1. Have students read the following verses and point out the qualities of meekness they present: Luke 6:29, 1 Peter 2:23 (non-resistance); Galatians 5:22–23 (fruit of the Spirit); 2 Timothy 2:25, Titus 3:2, 1 Peter 3:4 (gentle, peaceful).

2. Discuss the promises presented in the following verses: Psalm 37:11, 147:6, 149:9.

Meekness and Rest

1. Read Matthew 11:28–30. Discuss the burden Jesus is talking about. (The word Jesus used here means "a load carried or toil borne to the point of exhaustion.")

2. Discuss what is meant by rest.

3. Read and discuss Exodus 33:14; Psalm 55:6, 116:7.

4. Discuss the three burdens Tozer talks about: pride, pretense and artificiality.

5. Discuss the importance of surrendering to Christ's rest. Use 2 Samuel 22:29–37.

Closing

1. Read together the prayer on page 116 of *The Pursuit of God.*

2. Assign Tozer chapter 10 and hand out the study guide questions for next week.

3. Close in prayer.

Tozer Chapter 10

The Sacrament of Living

A sacrament is defined as a "formal, symbolic religious rite, especially the Christian ceremonies of baptism and the Eucharist." Tozer uses the word in his chapter title: "The Sacrament of Living." What does he mean? How can living be a sacrament?

The Sacred and the Secular

One of the greatest hindrances to a Christian's internal peace, according to Tozer, is "the common habit of dividing our lives into two areas—the sacred and the secular." Why is the habit of dividing our lives into sacred and secular such a hindrance to our peace? To answer this question we need to think about the ways in which we divide our lives. The following verses will stimulate your thinking: 1 John 2:15; James 4:4, 1:8; Psalm 73:25. Reread Tozer's words on pages 118 and 119:

> This tends to divide our total life into two depart-
> ments. We come unconsciously to recognize two sets of
> actions. The first are performed with a feeling of satis-
> faction and a firm assurance that they are pleasing to
> God. These are the sacred acts and they are usually

thought to be prayer, Bible reading, hymn singing, church attendance and such other acts as spring directly from faith. They may be known by the fact that they have no meaning whatever except as faith shows us another world, "an house not made with hands, eternal in the heavens" (2 Cor. 5:1).

Over against these sacred acts are the secular ones. They include all of the ordinary activities of life which we share with the sons and daughters of Adam: eating, sleeping, working, looking after the needs of the body and performing our dull and prosaic duties here on earth. These we often do reluctantly and with many misgivings, often apologizing to God for what we consider a waste of time and strength. The upshot of this is that we are uneasy most of the time. We go about our common tasks with a feeling of deep frustration, telling ourselves pensively that there's a better day coming when we shall slough off this earthly shell and be bothered no more with the affairs of this world.

This is the old sacred-secular antithesis. Most Christians are caught in its trap. They cannot get a satisfactory adjustment between the claims of the two worlds. They try to walk the tight rope between two kingdoms and they find no peace in either. Their strength is reduced, their outlook confused and their joy taken from them.

I believe this state of affairs to be wholly unnecessary. We have gotten ourselves on the horns of a dilemma, true enough, but the dilemma is not real. It is a creature of misunderstanding. The sacred-secular antithesis has no foundation in the New Testament. Without doubt, a more perfect understanding of Christian truth will deliver us from it.

Walk as Jesus Did

Read First John 2:6. If we are to walk as Jesus did, we must decide what that means. How did Jesus walk? How should He be our model?

Read John 8:28–29. These verses seem to indicate that His whole life was pleasing to the Father. What can we learn from that?

Read First Corinthians 10:31. So that's the answer. But how can we put into practice the command of First Corinthians 10:31? How do we practice living to the glory of God? Read Deuteronomy 10:12 and Matthew 5:16. How does "walking as Jesus did" relate to the following:

- our work?
- our relationships—spouse, children, friends, neighbors, etc.?
- our entertainment?
- our attitudes?

Living to the Glory of God

We must practice "living to the glory of God." That is not always easy. How can we increase our day-to-day awareness of living to the glory of God?

Tozer has a few suggestions:

1. Meditate on this truth each day: "I want to live today for God's glory!"
2. Talk to God often in prayer about this desire. Do this as often throughout the day as you can remember.
3. Try to recall it to mind frequently as you move about your day. Place little reminders ("Live a life to glorify God" written on cards) around—in your car, on your desk, etc.—anywhere you would regularly see them.

Tozer concludes: "Keep reminding God in [your] times of private prayer that [you] mean every act for His glory; then supplement those times by a thousand thought-prayers as [you] go about the job of living. Let us practice the fine art of making every work a priestly ministration. Let us believe that God is in all our simple deeds and learn to find Him there" (p. 123).

Holy Days and Rituals

Next, Tozer talked about the importance to the people of Israel of holy days and rituals. It is important to think about this issue and its purpose. Why did God bring about rituals and holy days in the worship practices of the Israelites? Tozer tells us on page 124 that it was not that God was teaching them that the holiness of things or places was important, but that *God is holy*. A second reason was that God wanted them to learn the difference between holy and unholy!

Tozer also points out that this Old Testament schooling was over when Christ came. What change made these rituals and symbolic days unnecessary? The veil was rent; we now have direct access to the Father. Read Hebrews 10:19–22. Everyone can enter in.

But what does that mean in relation to our worship? How is our worship to be different from that of the Old Testament? Read John 4:21–24 and meditate on its significance to our worship today.

Every Aspect a Holy Act

Making our whole life glorifying to God is not easy. But it is important to our spiritual growth. How does a person make every part of his or her life a holy, uncommon act? Tozer says:

> The motive is everything. Let a man sanctify the Lord God in his heart and he can thereafter do no common

act. All he does is good and acceptable to God through Jesus Christ. For such a man, living itself will be sacramental and the whole world a sanctuary. His entire life will be a priestly ministration. As he performs his never-so-simple task, he will hear the voice of the seraphim saying, "Holy, Holy, Holy, is the Lord of hosts: the whole earth is full of his glory." (p. 127)

LESSON PLAN—Group Study

AIM: To have my students realize that every aspect of their lives should be an act of worship that brings glory to God.

This lesson does not have as many Scripture passages as the other lessons. That means that discussion questions will play a much more vital role than in previous weeks.

Introduction

1. Open with prayer.

2. Discuss what a sacrament is. Why does Tozer title his chapter "The Sacrament of Living"?

The Sacred and the Secular

1. Use the following questions to stimulate discussion. What, according to Tozer, is one of the greatest hindrances to a Christian's internal peace? Why is the habit of dividing our lives into sacred and secular such a hindrance to our peace?

2. Have your students list some ways/areas where we separate the sacred and the secular.

3. Read the following verses and discuss their implications: 1 John 2:15; James 4:4, 1:8; Psalm 73:25.

4. Read the Tozer quote from pages 118 and 119. Discuss.

Walk As Jesus Did

1. Read First John 2:6. Discuss what it means to walk as Jesus did.

2. Read and discuss John 8:28–29.

3. Read First Corinthians 10:31. Discuss how we can practice living to the glory of God. Use Deuteronomy 10:12 and Matthew 5:16 for further discussion. Ask: How does "walking as Jesus did" relate to the following:

- our work?
- our relationships—spouse, children, friends, neighbors, etc.?
- our entertainment?
- our attitudes?

Living to the Glory of God

1. Discuss the concept of "living to the glory of God." How can we increase our day-to-day awareness of living to the glory of God? Use Tozer's suggestions:

A. Meditate on this truth each day: "I want to live today for God's glory!"
B. Talk to God often in prayer about this desire. Do this as often throughout the day as you can remember.
C. Try to recall it to mind frequently as you move about your day. Place little reminders ("Live a life to glorify

God" written on cards) around—in your car, on your desk, etc.—anywhere you would regularly see them.

Holy Days and Rituals

1. Discuss the importance of holy days and rituals in the Old Testament. Why did God bring them about?

2. Discuss what changed to make these unnecessary when Christ came. Read Hebrews 10:19–22.

3. Discuss how our worship is to be different from that of Old Testament Hebrews. Read John 4:21–24 and discuss the implications to worship.

4. Discuss: Does this mean we should not celebrate some rituals or special "holy days"? What is good about them? Do they ever become harmful in any way?

Every Aspect a Holy Act

1. Discuss how a person can make every aspect of his or her life a holy, uncommon act. Use Tozer quote from page 127.

Closing

1. Read together the prayer on pages 127–128 of *The Pursuit of God.*

2. Close with prayer.

Review

The Pursuit of God

(This lesson is for the group study only.)

This lesson is designed if you wish to have a review at the end of your study. The aim is simply to discern what impact the lessons have had on your students and to review the main points again.

Class Testimonies

The best review might be to allow students to share with each other what this study has done for them. Asking them to share a significant lesson the Lord taught them, or the most important thing they learned through the study, can be great discussion starters. Allow as much time as you need for this valuable exercise.

Review

Feel free to emphasize the points you feel are most needed. What is provided are simply the major points each chapter made and some statements or related Scriptures about each point.

Chapter 1—Following Hard after God

• God puts within us the impulse to pursue Him. It is our job to do the pursuing.

• You cannot know someone personally and intimately through one visit. Too many Christians stop at their initial finding and have no knowledge of intimacy.

• Philippians 3:4–14.

• Read what Tozer says about complacency on page 17.

Chapter 2—The Blessedness of Possessing Nothing

• We want to hold onto things, relationships, etc. We want to stay in control rather than to recognize that all things are God's.

• Mark 8:34–38; Luke 9:57–62.

• We want a gospel of convenience, but we must give everything to God's control!

Chapter 3—Removing the Veil

• We are created to glorify God. How can we? By walking in truth, maintaining the unity of body, disciplining our bodies, obeying God, keeping pure, doing good deeds before non-Christians, being prepared to suffer.

• Presented the idea that we can enter into God's presence. Hebrews 10:19–23.

• What hinders us? Sin, "self."

• Read Tozer quote from pages 44–45.

Chapter 4—Apprehending God

• There are different levels of belief.

• A true believer knows the reality of God in personal experience.

• The unregenerated person cannot apprehend God; we can.

• 1 Corinthians 2:6–16.

• Faith is the key—Hebrews 11:6.

• We must be "other-worldly." Use Tozer quote on pages 56–57.

Chapter 5—The Universal Presence

• God is everywhere; His presence is universal. But the manifestations of that presence are not always readily seen.
• What must we do in order to sense His presence? Use Tozer quote from page 64.
• Requires a complete surrender and a life of obedience to His Word.
• We must develop "spiritual receptivity."

Chapter 6—The Speaking Voice

• The aspects of God's spoken and written Word (powerful, purifies, eternal, food, written on our hearts, must love it, it brings light).
• We must be silent to hear. Use Tozer quote from page 80.
• We also must act in obedience to God's voice and we must exercise spiritually in order to hear it more often.

Chapter 7—The Gaze of the Soul

• Faith is defined functionally. There is always an action.
• Hebrews 11.
• James 2:14–26. Faith/works: if we truly have faith, the works will be there!
• How do we obtain faith? Ephesians 2:8; Romans 10:17.

Chapter 8—Restoring the Creator-Creature Relation

• Salvation restores the relationship. 2 Corinthians 5:17.
• The only right relation between us and God is full Lordship on His part and complete submission on our part.
• The proof of what or whom we are serving is in our daily choices.

• Only by truly exalting and honoring God is a proper relationship developed.

Chapter 9—Meekness and Rest

• What meekness means—a sense of humility.
• Matthew 11:28–30—the relationship of burdens and rest.
• God wants to relieve us of our burdens: pride, pretense, artificiality.
• We must recognize our complete dependency on Him to experience rest.

Chapter 10—The Sacrament of Living

• Our very life should be an offering of worship to God.
• We need to increase our day-to-day awareness of living to the glory of God.

Conclusion

• How do we know if we have a real relationship with God? The proof is in the fruit we bear. Read John 15:1–17. We all should look back from time to time to see what fruit there is.

INTRODUCTION QUESTIONNAIRE

Please answer these questions honestly. The answers are for your benefit alone.

1. How does one become a Christian?

2. When did I become a Christian?

3. Did becoming a Christian bring any noticeable changes to my life? What were they?

4. Have I ever had a subsequent experience that I would consider to be the filling of the Holy Spirit? When did it happen? What changes did this experience bring in my life?

5. Do I find joy in worshiping God, both privately and with fellow believers?

6. How often do I gather with other believers?
   a. less than weekly
   b. weekly
   c. twice a week
   d. more than twice a week

7. How often do I read my Bible?
   a. never
   b. seldom
   c. once or twice a week
   d. three to five times a week
   e. daily or oftener

8. How often do I converse with God in prayer?
   a. seldom
   b. once or twice a week
   c. three to five times a week
   d. daily
   e. frequently throughout the day

9. When I pray is it a meaningful time of communion, or do I quickly run through a list of requests?

10. When a problem occurs in my life, what is my first response to it?

  a. pray or ask "what is God trying to teach me?"
  b. immediately turn it over to God
  c. think "what am I going to do?"
  d. react emotionally
  e. do nothing

11. If I answered c, d or e to question 10, how soon do I get around to a or b?

  a. very quickly
  b. somewhat soon
  c. not very soon
  e. never

STUDY GUIDE QUESTIONS
SESSION 2
Chapter 1: Following Hard after God

1. What does the law of prevenient grace say in practical terms about our seeking God?

2. What is the essence of genuine religion? (John 17:3)

3. Why can't this intimate relationship with God come through our involvement with a body of believers?

4. In what way is the Christian life a paradox?

5. What is deadly to spiritual growth? Why?

6. In what ways does Tozer feel that we need simplicity in our spiritual life?

7. God is speaking to me through this chapter. The one thing I am going to do to develop a closer relationship with Him is:

The steps I am going to take to do this are:

STUDY GUIDE QUESTIONS

SESSION 3

Chapter 2: The Blessedness of Possessing Nothing

1. Tozer had a unique meaning for "poor in spirit." In your own words explain what he feels it means.

2. Read Genesis 22:1–18. While we often look at this passage as Abraham's test of faith, Tozer uses it to stress his point about placing God first in one's life. How does this incident support that point?

3. Why is clinging to things one of the most harmful habits in life?

4. What are some things that are hard for people to give up?

5. What things are hard for me to give up?

6. Read Matthew 19:16–30. What lessons from this passage relate to the theme of the chapter?

7. For further study look at the following passages of Scripture and summarize how each relates to our theme.

Mark 8:34–38:

Luke 9:57–62:

Luke 12:15–34:

Luke 14:26–35:

8. God is speaking to me through this chapter. The one thing I am going to do to develop a closer relationship with Him is:

The steps I am going to take to do this are:

STUDY GUIDE QUESTIONS

SESSION 4

Chapter 3: Removing the Veil

1. For what was mankind chiefly created?

2. In what areas does your life glorify God? In what areas does your life fail to glorify God?

3. What veil has now been removed? What does its removal mean for me as a Christian?

4. According to Tozer, what hinders Christians from entering into the presence of God? In what ways might this hindrance be present in your own life?

5. God is speaking to me through this chapter. The one thing I am going to do to develop a closer relationship with Him is:

The steps I am going to take to do this are:

STUDY GUIDE QUESTIONS

SESSION 5

Chapter 4: Apprehending God

1. "To most people God is an inference, not a reality." Is He a reality to you? If so, explain why and how He is real to you. If not, what could He do to make Himself a reality to you?

2. In what ways can we apprehend God in the same way we can apprehend this world?

3. Why can't unregenerate people apprehend God? (1 Corinthians 2:14; Romans 1:20–21)

4. What is the key for believers to know and have a habitual, conscious communion with God? In other words, what enables our spiritual senses to function? (Hebrews 11:6)

5. What is the difference between imagination and faith?

6. Why do we habitually think of the visible world as real and doubt the reality of the other?

7. What do we have to be if we truly seek to follow Christ?

8. God is speaking to me through this chapter. The one thing I am going to do to develop a closer relationship with Him is:

The steps I am going to take are:

STUDY GUIDE QUESTIONS
SESSION 6
Chapter 5: The Universal Presence

1. Explain in your own words the difference between pantheism and the doctrine of the divine Presence.

2. As an exercise of encouragement, rewrite Psalm 139:7–10 in your own words, substituting places and situations (i.e., work, the market, etc.) that are meaningful to you.

3. Why do some persons "find" God in a way others do not? What is "spiritual receptivity" and what does it have to do with why some have deep experiences and others struggle constantly in the "half-light of imperfect Christian experience"?

4. How does Psalm 27:8 relate to why some people have spiritual receptivity and others do not?

5. What does a person need to do to become more spiritually receptive?

6. God is speaking to me through this chapter. The one thing I am going to do to develop a closer relationship with Him is:

The steps I am going to take are:

STUDY GUIDE QUESTIONS

SESSION 7

Chapter 6: The Speaking Voice

1. What do Psalm 33:6, 9, Hebrews 11:3 and Genesis 1:9 indicate about the power of God's Word?

2. What is the relation of God's spoken Word to His written Word—the Bible?

3. How is God's voice apparent to even the unsaved? (John 1:9-10; Romans 1:20, 2:15)

4. In what ways is God's voice apparent to those who are His children?

5. Has there been a time in your life when you heard His voice? How did you know it was the voice of the Lord?

6. Read Psalm 29. What insights about God's voice can you glean from this passage?

7. How can we develop our sensitivity so we can more clearly and regularly "hear" God's voice?

8. God is speaking to me through this chapter. The one thing I am going to do to develop a closer relationship with Him is:

The steps I am going to take to do this are:

STUDY GUIDE QUESTIONS
SESSION 8
Chapter 7: The Gaze of the Soul

1. Read Hebrews 11:6. In light of this verse and what Tozer says, what do we have if we possess faith?

2. According to Hebrews 11:1, what is faith? Explain it in your own words.

3. What does Tozer mean when he says that faith is defined functionally, not philosophically?

4. How do we obtain faith? (Ephesians 2:8; Romans 10:17)

5. Explain the similarities and differences between the faith of a believer today and that of an Old Testament Israelite.

6. In what ways is faith a virtue that does not regard the self?

7. How does the development of individual faith help the unity of the body of Christ?

8. God is speaking to me through this chapter. The one thing I am going to do to develop my relationship with Him is:

The steps I am going to take are:

STUDY GUIDE QUESTIONS
SESSION 9

Chapter 8: Restoring the Creator-Creature Relation

1. Explain the importance of a "fixed center against which everything else is measured." Why should God be our fixed center?

2. According to Tozer, from where does much of our difficulty as seeking Christians stem? Why does this cause difficulty?

3. What does Tozer mean when he says "we must of necessity be servant to someone"?

4. What results from our truly exalting and honoring God?

5. God is speaking to me through this chapter. The one thing I am going to do to develop my relationship with Him is:

The steps I am going to take to do this are:

STUDY GUIDE QUESTIONS
SESSION 10
Chapter 9: Meekness and Rest

1. According to Tozer, what springs directly from our sins?

2. In Matthew 11:28–30 burden and rest are contrasted. What does each mean in these verses?

3. In what ways does Tozer indicate that one of the causes of our burden is pride?

4. What are the characteristics of a meek person?

5. Explain the other two causes of our burden.

6. God is speaking to me through this chapter. The one thing I am going to do to develop my relationship with Him is:

The steps I am going to take are:

STUDY GUIDE QUESTIONS
SESSION 11

Chapter 10: The Sacrament of Living

1. What, according to Tozer, is one of the greatest hindrances to a Christian's internal peace? Why is it such a hindrance?

2. In what way is Christ our model in overcoming this problem?

3. How can we put into practice the command of First Corinthians 10:31?

4. How do we practice living to the glory of God?

5. What, according to Tozer, was the purpose of the holy days and rituals of the Old Testament? And why does Tozer feel no great emphasis should be placed on such things today?

6. How does a person make every part of his life a holy, uncommon act?

7. God is speaking to me through this chapter. The one thing I am going to do to develop my relationship with Him is:

The steps I am going to take are: